Do You Want to Be an

Ancient Egyptian

Princess?

Written by
Jacqueline Morley

Illustrated by
Nicholas Hewetson

BOOK HOUSE

This edition first published in MMXV by Book House

Distributed by Black Rabbit Books
P.O. Box 3263
Mankato
Minnesota MN 56002

Cataloging-in-Publication Data is available
from the Library of Congress

ISBN: 978-1-909645-33-2

Series created and designed by David Salariya

Carolyn Graves-Brown, Fact Consultant
Curator of the Egypt Centre at the University of Wales Swansea

Photographic credits

The Art Archive / Egyptian Museum Turin / Dagli Orti: 9
The Art Archive / Egyptian Museum Cairo / Dagli Orti: 11
The Art Archive / Staatliche Sammlung Ägyptischer Kunst
Munich / Dagli Orti: 15
The Art Archive / Staatliche Sammlung Ägyptischer
Kunst Munich / Dagli Orti: 17
The Art Archive / Egyptian Museum Cairo / Dagli Orti: 27

The Art Archive / Luxor Museum / Dagli Orti: 29
The Art Archive / Dagli Orti: 22

Every effort has been made to trace copyright holders. The
Salariya Book Company apologizes for any unintentional
omissions and would be pleased, in such cases, to add an
acknowledgment in future editions.

Princess Needed

How would you like to become a member of the royal family of ancient Egypt?

The royal household, based in Thebes, has a vacancy for a princess with an interest in maintaining the glory of the ancient kingdom of Egypt.

Your main duties will include:

- obeying every wish of your father, the king, known as the pharaoh, who is a god on earth

- behaving at all times with the dignity expected of the daughter of a god

- avoiding any jealousy or plotting that may occur among the members of your family

Apply in writing to the pharaoh's chief minister, the vizier.

(An interest in all aspects of ancient Egyptian life would be an advantage.)

Contents

What Applicants Should Know

Be prepared for a journey back in time—to more than 3,000 years ago. The map below shows your destination, in the northeastern corner of Africa. Notice how the River Nile flows the whole length of the land. A strip on either side of the river is lush and green while all the rest of Egypt is desert. This is because the river floods its banks each year, watering the nearby land and coating it with thick, rich black mud. This flood makes the soil fertile so that crops grow plentifully and the country is rich. The wealth is very unevenly distributed. Most of it goes to the ruling pharaoh.

Ancient Egypt, c. 2000 B.C.

Ancient Egypt

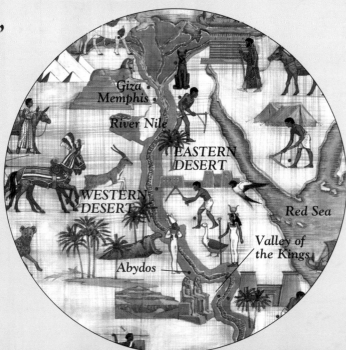

Giza
Memphis
River Nile
EASTERN DESERT
WESTERN DESERT
Red Sea
Valley of the Kings
Abydos

Your New Workplace

Imagine that you have woken up in an ancient Egyptian palace. You have servants to wait on you. When you go out they follow you, holding tall ostrich plumes to protect you from the fierce Egyptian sun. Inside the palace the great reception halls are richly decorated with painted scenes from nature. Here your father, the pharaoh, sees his ministers and guests. Beyond are the smaller rooms in which he lives. You do not enter these unless your father sends for you.

Royal family

Pharaoh

Queen

Royal children

In the palace garden

▼ You have a leafy garden with palm trees and a pool. Beyond the walls lies the hot, dusty, and crowded city.

Wasn't the vizier looking cross this morning!

◄ You will have to get used to the idea that your father is a god. Everyone believes that each pharaoh is Horus, the son of Osiris, ruler of the Land of the Dead. But pharaohs are also human, and when he has time, your father enjoys being with his family.

Lots of leisure time

▼ You often go to the garden to talk with your mother, the queen. As queens do not normally take an active part in government, she may spend quite a lot of time there.

We should be careful. He may be plotting something.

▶ The vizier, with his own secretary and fan-bearer, is your father's chief minister. He visits the palace daily. All other ministers report to him and he advises the pharaoh. He might even have a say in choosing a husband for you.

People in the palace

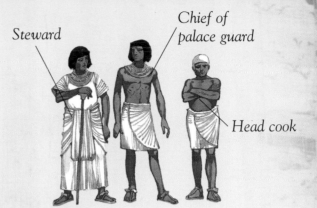

Steward

Chief of palace guard

Head cook

▲ Hundreds of servants work in the palace. Above are some of the most important ones.

Treasurer

Keeper of public records

Commander of the army

▲ These are some of the ministers who keep your father's government running smoothly. In theory, he does everything himself, since he is a god. In practice they do the hard work.

Vizier

Fan-bearer

Secretary

The Royal Household

You live in the women's part of the palace with your father's wives, young sons, and daughters. A pharaoh has several wives, though most of his subjects have just one. Your mother is the chief wife, the only one with the title of queen, so you are the most important daughter. Your little brother is heir to the throne but there are a few wives with older sons. This can cause jealousy and plotting. If anything were to happen to your father, a crafty wife would try to get her son made pharaoh. She might try to marry him to you—a pharaoh is allowed to marry his sister or half-sister.

Brothers and sisters galore

▼ You are never short of company in the women's quarters. The royal sons are also brought up there until they are about nine. There are lots of servants who look after the children.

> Did you win again, you clever boy? You are a marvel!

> I'm sure his mother bribes her to say things like that.

Royal babies

▶ Women who have breastmilk (because they have just had a baby) are hired to breast-feed the royal babies.

Woman breast-feeding

Royal wife with children

Ambitious wives

▶ This wife is very cunning. She wants to make her son the favorite child of the pharaoh and will use trickery to achieve her goal.

Your room in the palace

The room you sleep in has painted walls and a small window, high up to keep out the sun's glare. The room may seem bare because the ancient Egyptians do not have much furniture. They have beds, low tables, chairs, and stools. Instead of wardrobes they have storage boxes. Poor people sleep on mats and only have a few all-purpose stools.

Footboard

Folding bed

Chair

▲ You sleep in a bed like this, with a mattress and linen sheets. Your feet go toward the raised footboard.

▲ A royal chair made of ebony and inlaid with ivory and gold is made especially for you. It's a smaller version of the chairs your parents use.

▶ You also have a carved stool in your room.

Stool

Your pets

Greyhound

Cat

Monkey

▲ Keeping pets under control is a job for the servants.

▶ Instead of a pillow, you sleep with a headrest. Raising your head keeps it cool and away from any scary creepy-crawlies.

Headrest

Clothes for the Job

Every day you wear the same thing—a tunic of thin white linen over a body-hugging white sheath-dress. For women and young girls, there are also loose dresses. Those who have to do hard work wear a sheath-dress by itself, a tunic dress, or just a skirt. Small children often go naked. Though the ladies of the court wear clothes like yours, it will still be easy to see you are a princess. The linen you wear is the finest of all. It takes a weaver nine months to make enough for one tunic, and you have hundreds of tunics.

Crowning glory

◀ Like most elegant people you have your head shaved and wear a wig. The best wigs are made of human hair. The worst are date-palm fiber—they don't look as good!

Ready to face the day

▼ Both men and women wear eye makeup to protect their eyes from the harsh glare of the sun. You would not be seen in public without it. It comes as pots of powdered mineral—green (from malachite) and black (from galena).

Grand designs

▶ For an official ceremony, put on grand jewelry, like this pendant of gold and semiprecious stones.

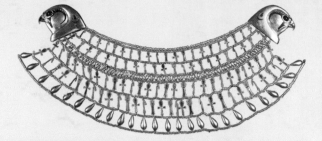

▲ Wide, beaded collars are very popular. Yours are made of gold, coral, or turquoise beads.

A well-groomed princess

A servant helps you dress in the morning and whenever you want to change. (The ancient Egyptians always look spotless, even those who do their own laundry, which means hand-washing in the river.) It helps to have someone to arrange the folds of your wide tunic, which is gathered and knotted at the chest. You often walk barefoot, carrying your sandals.

Wear green eye shadow made from malachite mixed with oil

Place a lotus bud in your headband

For special occasions, your wigs will have ringlets or braids

That gray powder is much too dark. Did you mix enough oil with it?

Your clothes are sprinkled with the perfume of crushed flowers

Sacred symbols

▶ The beetle on this armband symbolizes Khepri, a sun god. Most jewelry has some powerful symbol to ward off evil spirits.

11

The Working Day

The first duties of the day are to wash and dress, put on your makeup, and visit your mother. The pharaoh might also like to see you before his official day begins. Then it is study time. All the royal daughters are taught together by a tutor.

In the afternoon there is usually a ceremony to attend— to welcome an ambassador or to present a new governor with his seal of office. These events often end with an evening feast. The best evenings are those that the pharaoh spends with his favorite wife and children. That includes you!

Official duties

▼ Your official duties are limited to taking part in court ceremonies. You stand near the throne while your father receives important visitors.

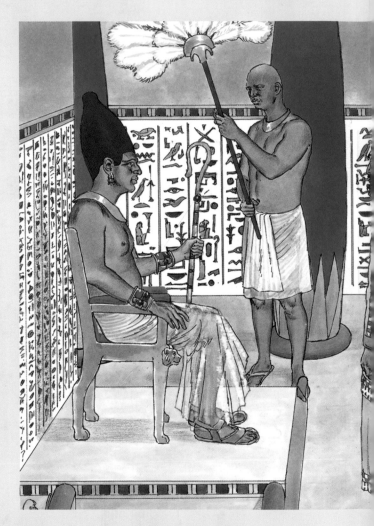

Musicians

◄ Listening to a professional musician in the women's quarters will help to pass the day.

The role of a princess

▲ If you had been the eldest prince, your tutors would be training you to govern, but princesses are not expected to rule. Attending ceremonial events like the one above is the only part you play in matters of state.

Behaving like a goddess

When your father gives a banquet, you eat with the guests. Always be dignified. You must act like the daughter of a god.

Clean and fresh

◄ Every morning you take a shower. You kneel in a trough and have water poured over you. Everyone washes daily, though there is no plumbing. Water is fetched from a well or the Nile.

I wonder where they came from—their clothes are so odd.

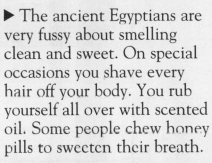

▶ The ancient Egyptians are very fussy about smelling clean and sweet. On special occasions you shave every hair off your body. You rub yourself all over with scented oil. Some people chew honey pills to sweeten their breath.

◄ Your servant brings you a freshly laundered tunic. It has hundreds of fine pleats. It has taken hours to put these in with a pleating board. When you are dressed you ask your servant how you look, because there are no full-length mirrors.

In ancient Egypt, men do all the professional work. Women are expected to look after the home. Poorer women have to work very hard. They help to grow the family's food, and they make things and sell them in the markets.

The Right Style

An Egyptian princess must obey the rules of proper behavior: always show respect and be obedient. It is believed that the gods once ruled on earth, setting the ways for people to live. So, you must not criticize the way things are done. If an elder tells you to do something, do not argue. Never give opinions unless asked. Despite these rules, ancient Egyptians enjoy life. They celebrate, and often joke about their betters behind their backs.

Performers at a royal feast

Flute

Lute

Zither

▲ Professional performers, often women, play music at a feast. This trio plays the lute, flute, and zither.

How to behave at a feast

▼ You should not stare at other guests or push forward to take food before your elders have had the chance to serve themselves.

Father has given a wonderful feast. The food is delicious!

▲ The pharaoh and queen have the seats of honor at a feast; you are the most important of the young ones. At first everyone is polite and proper, but soon people loosen up, laughing and calling for wine.

A feast for a pharaoh

A menu for a feast:
Bread in fancy shapes
Barley porridge
Roast fish
Pigeon stew
Roast quail
Spit-grilled kidney
Ribs of beef
Stewed figs
Honey cakes
Cheese
Wine

Seating arrangements

▼ You do not eat at a table. People sit on low chairs or on mats. It is perfectly polite to eat with your fingers.

> Let me drink to the health of the pharaoh and his queen

◄ The food is put out beside the guests, who help themselves.

Drinking vessel

▼ When everyone has eaten and feels contented, entertainers give an acrobatic dancing display.

Keeping fresh at the feast

At the start of the feast a servant will offer you a cone of scented wax for your head. The melting wax trickles down your face and wig and keeps you smelling fresh all evening.

Dancers

Getting Along without Money

Money does not exist in ancient Egypt. Instead of using coins, people do their shopping by swapping things that are of equal value: for example, three fresh fish and a wooden bowl for a pair of sandals. (This is called bartering.) The pharaoh is very rich because he owns everything in Egypt. He has vast buildings filled with precious objects. As the pharaoh's daughter, you can have anything you want.

The royal workshops

▼ The royal workshops make all the palace furniture, decorated with ivory and gold. They also make the painted and gilded statues, and all the precious palace vessels.

What do you think? The stone isn't very big.

▲ Everything the palace uses is made or grown on the royal estates. Ordinary people shop for what they need at market stalls. This woman (*above*) is offering a beaded necklace to pay for some fruit.

Jewels for a princess

Don't expect glittering diamonds and sapphires. These are not found in ancient Egypt. Instead, jewelers use semiprecious stones: amethyst, carnelian, jasper, turquoise, and deep blue lapis lazuli.

A new ring

▼ Your jewelry is also made in the workshops. The craftsmen's salary is paid in food and fine linen cloth.

Don't worry—that's the sign of Horus. It will keep you safe.

Most fine jewelry is set in gold, which comes from mines in the desert, east of the Nile. Silver has to be imported from other countries, so it is more highly prized than gold.

Metal and stone craftsmen

▼ The royal craftsmen work to the highest standards. Overseers check each stage of the work, which follows traditional designs. Painters and sculptors are not expected to produce anything new or unusual. As always in ancient Egypt, the old ways of doing things are believed to be the best.

Bellows

Coppersmiths smelting ore

▲ To make sure the fire stays hot enough, a man pumps the bellows with his feet.

Pouring molten gold

▶ The skills of ancient Egyptian goldsmiths are famous. The two at the top right are pouring molten gold into a mold to shape it. The others are hammering sheet gold into shape over blocks of wood.

Hammering sheet gold

Drill

◀ This man is making a vase from porphyry, a very hard stone. He hollows it out with a drill.

Porphyry vase

Opportunities for Travel

The pharaoh often leaves his capital, Memphis, to check how distant parts of his kingdom are being run. He will travel along the Nile. It is best to travel by river as all important places are near it. Nobody lives far from the river. Beyond its fertile banks there is nothing but desert. Important members of the pharaoh's family and court go with him. He takes his favorite wife and daughter, so you enjoy many river trips.

The Nile: Egypt's highway

▼ Many sorts of boats use the river: big trading vessels bringing goods from far away; little fishing boats, made from papyrus reeds, as well as pleasure boats.

Egyptian cargo boat

A pharaoh's judgment

▲ The pharaoh visits every province and hears petitions from local people. His subjects have the right to appeal to him to judge their case if they feel that the court in their hometown has treated them unfairly.

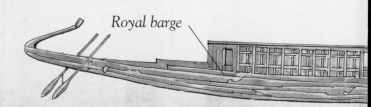

Royal barge

A river of history

▼ You glide past villages and temples and marvel at the enormous pyramids. These are royal tombs of long ago, built many centuries before your father's time.

Life by the river

It hardly ever rains, and without the Nile the land would be desert. As the annual flood retreats, it leaves water in a network of canals that crisscross the land. These are constantly repaired to keep them watertight. They must provide the farmers with water until the following year.

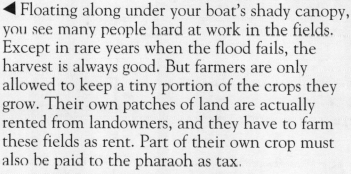

People harvesting crops along the Nile

◀ Floating along under your boat's shady canopy, you see many people hard at work in the fields. Except in rare years when the flood fails, the harvest is always good. But farmers are only allowed to keep a tiny portion of the crops they grow. Their own patches of land are actually rented from landowners, and they have to farm these fields as rent. Part of their own crop must also be paid to the pharaoh as tax.

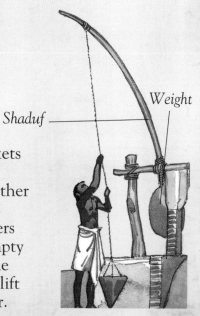

Shaduf ———

Weight

▶ Along the river, buckets hang from poles with counterweights at the other end. This mechanism is called a "shaduf." Farmers pull the ropes to dip empty buckets in the river. The counterweight helps to lift the full buckets of water.

At the Temple

Noble ladies of ancient Egypt also serve as priestesses in the temples. You do not have many duties, but it is a great honor to perform them.

Egypt is full of temples—at least one in each town and huge temples in the cities. Ancient Egyptians are very religious. They honor the gods on holy days and include them in all decisions they make every day.

Inside a temple

The gate leading to the temple opens onto a courtyard where townspeople leave offerings for the gods. Only priests and priestesses are allowed to enter the temple itself.

▲ The image of a god is kept in the innermost part of a temple. On holy days it is paraded through the streets, always covered because it is too sacred to be seen by ordinary people. Priests dress the image and offer it food daily, as if it were alive.

Painted temples

▶ Temples have massive stone walls decorated with carved and painted scenes.

Obelisk

Music for the gods

▼ You join in the sacred dancing in the vast, pillared temple hall. You make music with a sistrum, a rattle that you shake to placate the gods. On holy days you are in the gods' procession.

When the musicians start, count to three and shake your sistrum in time with me.

— Obelisk

◄ Tall obelisks, inscribed with hieroglyphs, stand beside an entrance gate.

Gods and goddesses

Hathor Horus Isis

Geb Re-Harakhty Osiris

Atum Khons Maat

▲ These gods seem fierce and strange, but to the ancient Egyptians they look stern and dignified. They display their special qualities in their appearance. Hathor is a loving goddess. She has the head of a cow because she overflows with the milk of kindness. Horus has a falcon's head. He is seen as the eye of the sun, like the falcon.

In Sickness and in Health

Life in ancient Egypt is not all sunshine and luxury—there are disadvantages. For example, desert sandstorms blow sand everywhere, even inside your palace. The sand in your food wears your teeth down. It inflames your eyes and dries your throat. People say that the desert is the home of demons and blame them for their bad luck. This can be worrying if you become seriously ill: your doctor will put his trust in amulets and spells to drive the evil spirits away.

A visit from the doctor

◄ When the doctor arrives he may be carrying a case made of cane and papyrus, like the one here. It holds his surgical instruments.

A relief showing a doctor's medical apparatus

Dangers to look out for

▼ Beware of dangers like crocodiles and venomous scorpions.

Plenty of rest, a simple diet, and spells three times a day for you.

Health risks

► You may get bad chest problems from breathing sand into your lungs during sandstorms.

Ancient medicine

▼ The doctor gives you a herb mixture and says a spell to make you well.

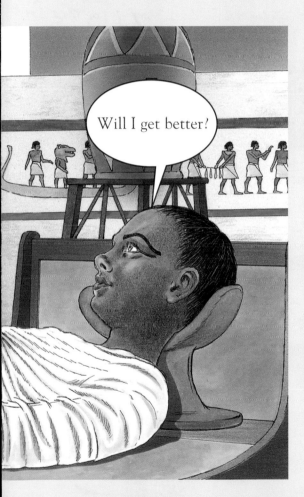

Will I get better?

When you are ill

▼ Doctors can do a lot for you if you are unwell. They can set broken bones and treat burns. They know a great deal about how the body works and how important a proper diet is. But they have not yet discovered germs, so they cannot treat serious diseases. If you are very ill, people will tell you to consult the famous healers of long ago. Statues are put up in their memory (*left*). You must place offerings before the statues and then beg the healers to cure you.

A statue of a male healer holding the image of Horus as a young boy

A charmed life

▲ The eye of Horus, shown on this amulet, is a very powerful charm to protect you against evil.

Locusts

Locust

▶ You may see people starve if locusts arrive. They land in swarms and devour all the crops.

Becoming a Queen

As the royal daughter, you are likely to be the next pharaoh's queen. You might marry your brother. The god Osiris married his sister Isis, so it is a godlike act for a pharaoh to marry his sister. Not all pharaohs and their subjects copy the customs of the gods. When you are queen you will hold court and attend long public ceremonies at the pharaoh's side. You must also be tactful with the other wives.

A royal honor

▼ As queen you help the pharaoh perform the ceremony of throwing gold. When the pharaoh wishes to honor someone for serving him well, he gives them gold.

A queen's tomb

▲ An Egyptian queen must have a magnificent tomb. Your tomb will be painted with scenes that have magical meanings. You give orders for this to your tomb painter.

▲ The ceremony is performed from a palace balcony. The royal children lend a hand. A great crowd gathers in the courtyard below, cheering as the gifts shower down—gold collars, rings, and armbands.

Who gets gold?

Usually a minister or official is rewarded, but important women can be honored, too.

River hunting boat

Throw-stick

Pharaoh rewards his loyal vizier!

Leisure time

▲ If the pharaoh enjoys your company you may join him when he hunts on the river. Its marshes are teeming with birds, which skillful hunters bring down with throw-sticks.

Protection for a princess

▼ When you travel through the city your bodyguards carry you in a litter. Everyone makes way for you.

Bodyguards

Litter

Could You Land the Top Job?

Your chances of being pharaoh are slim. Even if a pharaoh has no sons, a daughter is not in line for the throne. A few queens have reigned briefly in troubled times when there was no clear heir. One queen, Hatshepsut, seized the throne in 1503 B.C. when her husband died and the next pharaoh was still a child. Hatshepsut refused to step down when he grew up. She ruled as pharaoh for more than twenty years, until her death.

Pleasing the gods

▲ Suppose by chance you became pharaoh. Remember that the existence of Egypt depends on you. You must rule in a way that pleases the gods or they will not send the flood that makes things grow.

Pharaoh at last

▼ Here you are, seated on the throne of Horus. Your subjects believe that the gods have put you there because everything happens exactly as the gods wish.

This is the first woman I have seen on the throne of Horus.

▲ Your commands are law. They are written down as you speak. You are chief judge in every court, chief priest of every temple. You make all decisions in government. Ministers and priests are merely there to help you.

A mighty pharaoh

▼ You wear a headdress decorated with the shape of a serpent. The rearing head of the serpent is a symbol for the sun god Re.

She looks as though she means to stay!

Going to war

▶ You are head of the army and must inspect your regiments. These are formed of archers, foot soldiers (*right*), and officers in chariots. As pharaoh, you must lead the way into battle, shooting arrows from your chariot as you hurtle toward the enemy.

Spear

Shield

Ax

Being a god, you cannot lose the battle (if you do, you make sure the news is kept secret). Hatshepsut did not lead her army personally, so perhaps you can get out of it, too.

The mark of a pharaoh

▶ Hatshepsut is shown (*right*) as a sphinx wearing the false beard, which is one of the emblems of a pharaoh.

Hatshepsut

Beard

Sphinx

Long-term Prospects

I f the proper preparations have been made, you will live forever in the Land of the Dead, a place ruled by the god Osiris. Like Egypt, it has a river and golden cornfields, but without any work or worry. You will not get there unless your ka is kept alive. Everyone has a ka. It is the spirit that inhabits your body. When you die your body must be specially preserved, so that it will last forever. It will be sealed in your tomb to provide a home for your ka.

We have to do the job properly for a royal mummy, but this Anubis mask makes it hot work.

Across the river

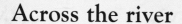 ▼ Your body will be made into a mummy and put on a boat-shaped bier (sled). Mourners will ferry it over the Nile to the tomb you had constructed on the western bank.

A royal burial

◀ This is your mummy in its case. The lid will be decorated with your portrait.

In the afterlife

▶ To ensure that you will be able to speak and eat in the next world, a ceremony called the Opening of the Mouth takes place. Priests burn incense and touch the mouth on your mummy case with sacred objects.

Thoth   Anubis   Maat

Monster

▶ Your body is now safely packaged; next you must enter the Hall of Judgment where the jackal-headed god Anubis weighs your heart. Maat, goddess of truth, watches and Thoth, god of writing, waits to note the result. If your heart is good and true it will balance with the Feather of Truth (Maat). A monster called the "Devourer" waits to gobble up the heavy hearts of wicked people. It has the head of a crocodile, the top half of a lion, and the back half of a hippo.

Mummy case lid

▲ Your body has been drying out in natron (a sort of salt) for many weeks, to stop it from rotting. The embalmers have packed it with spices to keep it sweet. Now they wrap it in layers of linen, with amulets between them to protect you from evil spirits.

Your Interview

Answer these questions to test your knowledge, then look at page 32 to find out if you have what it takes to get the job.

Q1   How many wives does your father have?
A   several
B   one
C   none

Q2   What do you wear at a feast?
A   a lump of wax
B   a sun hat
C   a headdress of porphyry

Q3   What is the best way to travel in ancient Egypt?
A   on foot
B   on a camel
C   in a boat

Q4   What does the pharaoh throw from his balcony?
A   rubbish
B   gold
C   grain

Q5   What does the pharaoh wear as a sign of kingship?
A   a false nose
B   a false beard
C   false eyelashes

Q6   What must your heart be like to enter the Land of the Dead?
A   as light as a feather
B   as heavy as lead
C   as black as night

Q7   When is the Opening of the Mouth ceremony performed?
A   when you are hungry
B   when you are very bored
C   when you are dead

Q8   Ka is the name of what?
A   your brother
B   your spirit
C   your favorite food

Glossary

Amulet. Small decorative object, worn or carried, which was thought to ward off evil.

Appeal. To ask a higher authority to decide if a court judgment is fair and correct.

Bier. Movable coffin-stand.

Carnelian. A red, semiprecious stone.

Galena. Lead ore.

Gilded. Covered with a layer of gold.

Hieroglyphs. A form of writing using picture symbols.

Lapis lazuli. Semiprecious stone with a dark blue color.

Linen. Fabric woven from the fibers of the flax plant.

Litter. Seat, with horizontal carrying poles, that bearers carried on their shoulders.

Malachite. A green mineral.

Molten. Melted by heat.

Obelisk. Four-sided tapering pillar of stone.

Petition. To make an official request for help from someone in authority.

Pleat. Flattened fold or crease in cloth.

Province. Region or division of a country.

Quail. Small edible bird related to the partridge.

Scorpion. Creature related to spiders, with a venomous sting in its tail.

Seal. Small object with an official sign cut into it.

Smelting. To extract metal from ore by melting.

Sphinx. A stone statue with the body of a lion and the head of a human.

Steward. An official responsible for running a household or estate.

Throw-stick. Shaped length of wood used to strike moving targets.

Zither. A plucked musical instrument.

Index

Have You Got the Job?

Count up your correct answers (*below right*) and find out if you got the job.

Your score:

8 Congratulations, you were made for the job.

7 Not quite ready to be a princess, but we can offer you a place as
a royal attendant.

5–6 Promising at the interview. We'll keep a note of your name.

3–4 Not prepared for this job. Try again later.

Fewer than 2 Are you sure you want to be an Egyptian princess?

1 (A) page 8
2 (A) page 15
3 (C) page 18
4 (B) page 24
5 (B) page 27
6 (A) page 29
7 (C) page 29
8 (B) page 28